Pastoral Cautions

ABRAHAM BOOTH

ABRAHAM BOOTH

1734 - 1806

Booth, Rev. Abraham, was born in Blackwell, Derbyshire, England, May 20, 1734. At ten years of age he was first made to feel a deep concern for his salvation. At twenty-one he was baptized among the General or Arminian Baptists. They encouraged him to preach among them....When it pleased God to open his eyes to see the whole truth he began to plan a work that would commend the doctrines of grace, and when he was about thirty-three years old he published his "Reign of Grace"....He was ordained pastor of the Prescott Street Church in London Feb. 16, 1769. He was a man of vast reading in his own language and in Latin, and he was justly reputed one of the most learned men of his day. He was instrumental in founding Stepney College, which has been such a blessing to the British Baptist churches. Mr. Booth was a man of strict integrity, of great devoutness, and of a large knowledge of the divine Word. Few men have served the cause of God by their writings, sermons, counsels, and example more effectively than Abraham Booth. He died Jan. 27, 1806, in his seventy-third year, after a pastorate of thirty-seven years in London. He was the author of eight works, besides a number of printed sermons.

—Adapted and lightly revised from William Cathcart, *The Baptist Encyclopedia* (Philadelphia: L. H. Everts, 1881), 114.

ABRAHAM BOOTH

PASTORAL CAUTIONS:

AN

ADDRESS

TO THE LATE

MR. THOMAS HOPKINS,

WHEN ORDAINED

PASTOR OF THE CHURCH OF CHRIST,

IN EAGLE STREET, RED LION SQUARE, LONDON,

JULY 13, 1785.

ABRAHAM BOOTH

The reminder of that exhortation of Paul, 'Take heed to yourself,'
wonderfully affected my mind; and this is the reason why I most
willingly call that to mind again for others as well.
A. H. FRANCK.

We must, in the first place, take heed to ourselves,
if we intend to take heed to the flock, as we ought.
DR. J. OWEN.

EDITED BY
QUINN R. MOSIER

BAPTIST HERITAGE PRESS
KANSAS CITY, MO

BH P

BAPTIST HERITAGE

PRESS

www.baptistheritagepress.org

First published 1805

Typeset in Adobe Caslon Pro at
Baptist Heritage Press, Kansas City

CONTENTS

EDITOR'S PREFACE

ll great books speak without respect to time. They are not held prisoner by their place in history, but break free from the chains that would confine them to a single generation. Great books stretch across the centuries, speaking to the heart of every man as though the author himself were living in our own times, with a lived understanding of our particular joys and sorrows. And because the heart of man remains the same throughout every age, the great books that address it remain timeless.

Booth's cautions for pastors are as relevant today as when he first preached them. A pastor for thirty-seven years, Booth speaks with lived insight into the joys and challenges of pastoral ministry. He has the brassy clarity of a prophet—mincing no words, cutting to the heart, and exposing every attempt at false piety. Yet for all the sharpness of his words, they also bind up and heal. Both those serving as pastors and those aspiring to the ministry would do well to read and pray through these cautions, asking whether there is not something in themselves that calls for repentance.

The occasion for this work was the installation service of Mr. Thomas Hopkins as pastor of the Baptist church in

Eagle Street, London. Dr. John Rippon preached the installation sermon, and Abraham Booth delivered the pastoral
charge, which is here reproduced as *Pastoral Cautions*. Hopkins had the precarious position of following Dr. Andrew Gifford, the church's first and only pastor up to that point, who
had served faithfully for fifty-four years. Hopkins supplied
the pulpit for three months preceding Gifford's death, which
prompted him to say of Hopkins, "That's the man for Eagle
Street."[1] Not everyone agreed. Soon after the beginning of
Hopkins' ministry, a faction of the church's wealthier members
withdrew, expressing dissatisfaction with his leadership and
preaching. Booth's words, spoken to Hopkins in the presence
of these very people, were prescient,

> "You may, it is highly probable, have painful opportunities
> of observing…your people…rambling about from one place
> of worship to another, admiring almost every fresh preacher
> they hear but quite dissatisfied with your ministry though they
> hardly know for what….You must guard, however, against de-
> sponding discouragement when any of these painful particu-
> lars occur to your notice" (35–36).

These members went only two miles west to Grafton Street
Baptist Church, where they helped fund the building of an
admirable meeting house. It is likely this group was in Booth's
mind when he cautioned Hopkins against showing partiality
to the wealthier members of the congregation in his charge.

Hopkins's ministry at Eagle Street was short and difficult.
He died only two years and four months after beginning as

---

[1] Joseph Ivimey, *A History of the English Baptists*, vol. 4 (London: Isaac Taylor Hinton, 1830), 341.

their pastor. After returning home one day in the rain from his public duties, he contracted a fever and passed away only a few days later. The final sermon he ever preached was from Hebrews 2:3: "How shall you escape, if you neglect so great a salvation."

Ever since its first printing in 1805, Booth's *Pastoral Cautions* has been useful to many ministers. Congregationalist minister John Angell James[2] said that he read Booth's charge so frequently in his early years of ministry that he could recite many portions of it by heart. He wrote, "I owe more to that small tract, than perhaps to any book, except the Bible. It is the best manual for pastors, for its size, that I am acquainted with."[3]

It is my prayer that everyone holding this book may be equipped for every good work to which the Great Shepherd and Overseer of souls has called you to. It is a fearful and awesome thing to watch over souls that have been bought with the blood of Jesus. May the words of Booth both humble and inspire you to deeper and truer devotion to the Lord Jesus, who knows the hearts of men—and most of all, the hearts of his ministers.

This text has been very lightly edited. Scripture references

---

[2] John Angell James (1785–1859) was an English Congregational minister who pastored at Carrs Lane Independent Chapel in Birmingham for fifty-four years. His fame grew in England as a preacher, even attracting a young Charles Spurgeon to go and hear him preach. His most known works are *The Anxious Inquirer* and *An Earnest Ministry*. He was a co-founder of the Evangelical Alliance and of the Congregational Union in England and Wales, as well as a famous abolitionist.

[3] John Angell James, "Affectionate Counsels to Students of Theology, On Leaving College, and Also to Young Ministers," in *The Works of John Angell James*, vol. 5 (London: Hamilton Adams & Co., 1860), 434.

have been added where appropriate, punctuation updated, and editorial footnotes included for further detail. These footnotes are indicated by brackets [...] so as not to be confused with Booth's original notes.

Soli Deo Gloria.

Quinn R. Mosier
Kansas City, Missouri

PASTORAL CAUTIONS

As you, my brother, are now invested with the pastoral office in this church and have requested me to address you on the solemn occasion, I shall endeavour to do it with all the freedom of a friend and with all the affection of a brother, not as your superior but as your equal.

The language of divine law on which I shall ground my address is that memorable injunction of Paul in his charge to Timothy, "Take heed to thyself" (1 Tim. 4:16).[1]

Very comprehensive, salutary, and important is this apostolic precept. For it comes recommended to our serious and submissive regard as the language of a saint who was pre-eminent among the most illustrious of our Lord's immediate followers, as the advice of a most accomplished and useful minister of the gospel when hoary with age, rich with experience, and almost worn down by arduous labours, and as the command of an apostle who wrote by the order and inspiration of Jesus Christ. This divine precept I shall now take the liberty of urging upon you in various points of light.

---

[1] See also, Acts 20:28.

———

1. Take heed to yourself, then, with regard to the reality of true godliness and the state of religion in your own soul. That you are a partaker of regenerating grace, I have a pleasing persuasion; that you have some experience of those pleasures and pains, of those joys and sorrows which are peculiar to real Christians, I make no doubt. But this does not supersede the necessity of the admonition. Make it your daily prayer and your diligent endeavour, therefore, to feel the importance of those truths you have long believed—of those doctrines you now preach. Often inquire at the mouth of conscience what you experience of their comforting, reproving, and sanctifying power. When you have been preaching the promises of grace or urging the precepts of duty, earnestly pray that their practical influence may appear in your own dispositions and conduct. Endeavour to realise the force and to comply with the requisition of that precept: "Grow in grace, and in the knowledge of our Lord and Saviour, Jesus Christ" (2 Pet. 3:18).

In proportion as the principles of true piety are vigorous in your heart, may you be expected to fill up the wide circumference of pastoral duty. For there is no reason to fear that a minister, if tolerably furnished with gifts, will be remarkably deficient or negligent in any known branch of pastoral obligation while his heart is alive to the enjoyments and duties of the Christian character. It is from the pastor's defects, considered under the notion of a disciple, that his principal difficulties

2

and chief dangers arise. For, my brother, it is only on the permanent basis of genuine Christian piety that your pastoral character can be established or appear with respectability in the light of the New Testament. I called genuine Christian piety *permanent* because everything essential to it will abide and flourish in immortal vigour, whereas the pastoral office, though honourable and important when connected with true godliness, must soon be laid aside as inconsistent with the heavenly state.

———

2. Take heed to yourself, lest you mistake an increase of gifts for a growth in grace. Your knowledge of the Scriptures, your abilities for explaining them, and your ministerial talents in general may considerably increase by reading, study, and public exercise, while real godliness is far from flourishing in your heart. For among all the apostolic churches, none seem to have abounded more in the enjoyment of spiritual gifts than the church at Corinth, yet few of them appear to have been in a more unhappy state or more deserving of reproof. I have long been of opinion, my brother, that no professors of the genuine gospel have more need to be on their guard against self-deception respecting the true state of religion in their own souls than those who statedly dispense the gracious truth. For as it is their calling and their business frequently to read their Bibles and to think much on spiritual things—to pray, and preach, and often to converse about the affairs of piety—they will, if not habitually cautious, do it all *ex officio*, or merely as the work of their ministerial calling, without feeling their own interest in it.

To grow in love to God and in zeal for his honour, in conformity to the will of Christ and in heavenly-mindedness, should be your first concern. Look well, therefore, to your internal character. For it is awful to think of appearing as a minister without being really a Christian, or of any one officially watching over the souls of others who is habitually unmindful of his own immortal interests.

In the course of your public ministry and in a great variety of instances, you may perhaps find it impracticable to enter into the true spirit of a precept or of a prohibition so as to reach its full meaning and its various applications, without feeling yourself convicted by it. In cases of this kind, you must fall under the conviction secretly before God and pray over it with undissembled contrition, agreeably to that saying, "Thou that teachest another, teachest thou not thyself?" (Rom. 2:21). When ministers hardly ever make this practical application of their public admonitions and cautions, as if their own spiritual interests were not concerned in them, their consciences will grow callous, and their situation with regard to eternity will be extremely dangerous. For this being habitually neglected, how can they be considered as walking *humbly* with God, which, nevertheless, is of such essential importance in the Christian life that without it all pretences to true piety are vain? Hence, an author[2] of no small repute in the churches of Christ says,

> "He that would go down to the pit in peace, let him keep up
> duties in his family and closet; let him hear as often as he can
> have opportunity; let him speak often of good things; let him
> leave the company of profane and ignorant men, until he have
> obtained a great repute for religion; let him preach, and labour
> to make others better than he himself; and, in the mean time,
> neglect to humble his heart to walk with God in a manifest
> holiness and usefulness, and he will not fail of his end."[3]

*3. Take heed that your pastoral office prove not a snare to
your soul by lifting you up with pride and self-importance.* Forget not that the whole of your work is ministerial, not legislative, that you are not a lord in the church, but a servant, that
the New Testament attaches no honour to the character of a
pastor except in connection with his humility, benevolence,
diligence, and zeal in promoting the cause of the Great Shepherd, and that there is no character upon earth which so ill
accords with a proud, imperious, haughty spirit as that of a
Christian pastor.

If not intoxicated with a conceit of your own wisdom and
importance, you will not, when presiding in the management
of church affairs, labour to have every motion determined

[2] [John Owen was a Puritan Nonconformist, theologian, and vice-chancellor of the University of
Oxford. His writings are voluminous and he is the crown jewel of Puritan minds.]

[3] Dr. Owen's Sermons and Tracts, p. 47. Folie. London, 1721. [John Owen, *The Works of John
Owen, D.D.*, vol. 16, ed. William Orme (London: Richard Baynes, 1826), 216.]

according to your own inclination. For this would savour of ecclesiastical despotism, be inconsistent with the nature and spirit of congregational order, and implicitly grasp at a much larger degree of power and responsibility than properly falls to your share.

Nor, if this caution be duly regarded, will you consider it as an insult on either your ministerial wisdom or your pastoral dignity if, now and then, one or another of your people, and even the most illiterate among them, should remind you of some real or supposed inadvertency or mistake, either in doctrine or conduct—no, not though it be in blunt language and quite unfounded. For a readiness to take offence on such occasions would be a bar to your own improvement and, perhaps, in articles relatively considered, of great importance. Nay, in such cases, to be soon irritated, though not inconsistent with shining abilities nor yet with great success in the ministry, would, nevertheless, be an evidence of pride and of your being as a Christian, in a poor, feeble state. For to be easily shoved out of the way, pushed down, as it were, with a straw, or caused to fall into sin by so feeble an impulse must be considered as an undoubted mark of great spiritual weakness (Rom. 15:1). Because the health of the soul and the vigour of the spiritual life are to be estimated not by our knowledge and gifts, but by the exercise of Christian graces, in cheerfully performing arduous labours, in surmounting successive difficulties, and in patiently bearing hardships for the sake of Jesus. Yes, and in proportion to the degree of your spiritual health will be your meekness and forbearance under those improprieties of treatment by one and another of your people, which you will undoubtedly meet. On examining ourselves by this rule, it will plainly appear, I presume, that though many of us in this assembly might, with regard to the length of our Christian profession, be justly denominated fathers, yet, with reference to spiritual stature and strength, we deserve no better character than that of ricketty children. Think not, however, that I advise you always to tolerate ignorant, conceited, and petulant professors in making exceptions to your ministry or in calling you to account for your conduct without reason and without good manners, but endeavour, with impartiality and prudence, to distinguish between cases of this kind. Then the simple and sincere, though improperly officious, will not be treated with resentful harshness but with some resemblance of what is beautifully denominated "the meekness and gentleness of Jesus Christ" (2 Cor. 10:1). But, alas! how poorly we imitate our Perfect Pattern!

It is of such high importance that a pastor possess the government of his own temper and a tolerable share of prudence when presiding in the management of church affairs that, without these, his general integrity, though undisputed, and his benevolence, though usually considered exemplary, will be in danger of impeachment among his people. Nay, notwithstanding the fickleness and caprice of many private professors with regard to their ministers, it has long appeared probable to me that a majority of those uneasinesses, animosities, and separations, which to the disgrace of religion take place between pastors and their several churches, may be traced up either to the unchristian tempers, to the gross imprudence, or to the laziness and neglects of the pastors themselves.

4. Take heed to yourself respecting your temper and conduct in general. Every one that calls himself a Christian should fairly represent, in his own dispositions and behaviour, the moral character of Jesus. The conversation of every professor should not only be free from gross defects, but it should be worthy of general imitation. But though each member of this church be under the same obligations to holiness as yourself, yet your spiritual gifts, your ministerial office, and your pastoral relation suggest a variety of motives to holiness that your people do not possess. Make it your diligent concern, therefore, to set your hearers a bright example, formed on that perfect model—the temper and conduct of Jesus Christ.

Yes, my brother, it is required that pastors, in their own persons and conduct, especially in the discharge of ministerial duties, give a just representation of the doctrine they preach and of Him in whose name they dispense it. But in order to do this, though in an imperfect manner, what integrity, benevolence, humility, meekness, and zeal for the glory of God; what self-denial and readiness for bearing the cross; what mortification of corrupt affections and inordinate desires of earthly things; what condescension and patience; what contempt of the world and heavenly-mindedness are necessary—not only the Scripture declares, but the nature of the thing shows.

Persons who are not acquainted with the true nature and genius of evangelical doctrine will always be disposed to charge the gospel itself with having a strong tendency to encourage those immoralities which appear in the character of its professors, and especially of those that preach it. Hence an apostle says, "Giving no offence in anything that the ministry be not blamed " (2 Cor. 6:3). For what can persons, otherwise uninformed, with more appearance of reason conclude than that the example of those who propagate the doctrine of salvation by grace through Jesus Christ is an authentic specimen of its genuine tendency in the hearts and lives of all those who believe and avow it? In the ministry of religious teachers there is an implicit language, which is commonly considered by their hearers as importing that what they do and are, if disgraceful, is the effect, not of their natural depravity or of peculiar temptations, but of their doctrinal principles. Hence, the ministers of Christ are commanded in all things to show themselves patterns of good works—to be examples to believers "in word, in conversation, in charity, in spirit, in faith, in purity" (1 Tim. 4:12). Yes, my brother, the honour and preferment to which our divine Lord calls his ministers are to give a just representation in their own conduct of the graces of his Person and the holiness of his doctrine to others. For whatever apparently splendid advantages a man may have with reference to the ministry, if they do not enable him the more effectually in his Christian course and ministerial work to express the humility, the meekness, the self-denial, and the zeal of the Chief Shepherd, together with the holiness of the doctrine he teaches, will redound but little to his account another day.[4]

I will now adopt the words of our Lord and say, "Take heed and beware of covetousness" (Luke 12:15). That evil turn of heart, which is here proscribed with such energy and such authority, is, through the false names it assumes and the pleas which it makes, to be considered as extremely subtle and equally pernicious. It evidently stands opposed in Scripture to contentment with the allotments of providence (Heb. 13:5), to spiritual mindedness (Luke 12:15–21), and to real piety (Col. 3:5, Eph. 5:5, 1 Cor. 5:11). It is an extremely evil disposition of the heart, of which, notwithstanding, very little account is made by the generality of those who profess the gospel of divine grace, except when it procures the stigma of penuriousness or the charge of injustice. But whatever excuses or palliatives may be invented, either to keep the consciences of covetous professors quiet or to support a good opinion of others respecting the reality of their piety, the New Testament declares them unworthy of communion in a church of Christ, and classes them with persons of profligate hearts and lives (2 Cor. 5:11, 6:9–10). The existence and habitual operation of this evil, therefore, must be considered as forming a character for hell (Psa. 10:3, 1 Cor. 6:10). Nor need I inform you that,

---

[4] See Dr. Owen's Nature of Apostasy, p. 441–444.

for a long course of ages, myriads of those who assumed the appellation of Christian ministers have been so notorious for an avaricious disposition, for the love of secular honours, and for the lust of clerical domination, as greatly to promote infidelity and expose Christianity to contempt.

———

5. *Take heed, then, and beware of covetousness.* For neither the comfort, the honour, nor the usefulness of "a man's life consisteth in the abundance of the things which he possesseth" (Luke 12:15). "Let your conversation be without covetousness," and, possessing the necessaries of life, without being indebted to any man, "be content with such things as ye have: for He," who governs the world, "hath said, I will never leave thee nor forsake thee" (Heb. 13:5). For as a man's happiness does not consist in *things*, but in *thoughts*, that abundance after which the carnal heart so eagerly pants is adapted to gratify not the demands of reason, much less the dictates of conscience, nor yet the legitimate and sober claims of appetite, but a fond imagination, pride of show, the love of secular influence, the lust of dominion, and a secret desire of lying as little as possible at the mercy of providence. I have somewhere seen it reported of Socrates, the prince of pagan philosophers, that on beholding a great variety of costly and elegant articles exposed to sale, he exclaimed, "How many things are here that I do not want!" So, my brother, when entering the abode

11

of wealth, we behold the stately mansion, the numerous ac-commodations, the elegant furniture, the luxurious table, the servants in waiting, and the fashionable finery of each indi-vidual's apparel, with what propriety and emphasis ought each of us to exclaim, "How many things are here which I do not want, which would do me no good, and after which I have no desire!" For we should not forget who it was that said, "How hardly shall a rich man enter the kingdom of heaven!" (Matt. 19:23).

I said, *possessing the necessaries of life without being indebted to any man.* For this purpose, resolutely determine to live, if practicable, within the bounds of your income; not only so as to keep out of debt, but, if possible, to spare something for the poor. Supposing, my brother, that either through the afflicting hand of God, or the criminal neglect of your people, unavoid-able straits approach, be not afraid of looking poverty in the face, as if it were, in itself considered, a disgraceful evil. For poverty is a very innocent thing, and absolutely free from de-served infamy, except when it is found in scandalous compa-ny. But if its forerunner and its associates be pride, laziness, a fondness for good living, a want of economy, and the contract-ing of debts without a probability of paying them, it deserves detestation, and merits contempt, and is inconsistent with vir-tuous conduct, and must gradually sink the character of any minister. If, on the contrary, it be found closely connected with humility and patience, with diligence, frugality, and integri-ty—such integrity as impels, for instance, to wear a threadbare coat, rather than run into debt for a new one; to live on the meanest wholesome food, or to go with half a meal, rather than contract a debt which is not likely to be discharged, such penury will never disgrace either the minister himself or the cause of Jesus Christ. Not the minister himself, because in the purest state of Christianity the most eminent servants of our divine Lord were sometimes distressed with want of both decent apparel and necessary food (2 Cor. 11:27; Acts 3:6). Not the cause of Jesus Christ, for his kingdom not being of this world, but of a spiritual nature, it cannot be either adorned by riches or disgraced by poverty. Besides, the ministers of evangelical truth must be poor indeed, if in humbler circumstances than Jesus himself was when proclaiming the glad tidings of his kingdom. It must, however, be acknowledged that, so far as a faithful pastor is reduced to the embarrassments of poverty merely by his people withholding those voluntary supplies which they were well able to have afforded, and to which, in common justice, equally as by the appointment of Christ he had an undoubted right (1 Cor. 11:1), the best of causes is disgraced and the offenders are exposed to severe censure.

Were a pastor driven to the painful alternative of either entering into some lawful secular employment or continuing his pastoral relation and stated ministrations in a course of embarrassment by debts, which he could not pay, the former would become his duty. Not only because we ought never to do evil that good may come, but also because it is much more evident that he ought to owe no man anything, that it is, that the Lord ever called him to the ministry or qualified him for it. But if necessity do not impel, the following passage seems to have the force of a negative precept respecting the Christian pastor: "No man that warreth entangleth himself with the affairs of this life, that he may please him who hath chosen him to be a soldier" (2 Tim. 2:4). A pastor should be very cautious, not only of entering unnecessarily into stated secular employment, but also of accepting any trust, though apparently advantageous, in which the preservation and the management of property are confided to his integrity and prudence. For so critically observed is the conduct of a man that has the management of another's pecuniary affairs, and so delicate is a minister's character, that he is in peculiar danger of exposing himself to censure and of injuring his public usefulness by such engagements.

———

6. Take heed, I will venture to add, take heed to your Second-Self in the person of your wife. As it is of high importance for a young minister in single life to behave with the utmost delicacy in all his intercourse with female friends, treating with peculiar caution those of them that are unmarried, and as it behoves him to pay the most conscientious regard to religious character when choosing a companion for life, so, when in the conjugal state, his tenderest attention is due to the domestic happiness and the spiritual interests of his wife.

This obligation, my brother, manifestly devolves upon you, as being already a husband and a father. Next after your own soul, therefore, your wife and your children evidently claim the most affectionate, conscientious, and pious care.

Nor can it be reasonably doubted that many a devout and amiable woman has given her hand to a minister of the gospel in preference to a private Christian, though otherwise equally deserving, in sanguine expectation, by so doing, of enjoying peculiar spiritual advantages in the matrimonial relation. But, alas! there is much reason to apprehend that not a few individuals among those worthy females have often reflected to the following effect:

"I have, indeed, married a preacher of the gospel, but I do not find in him the affectionate domestic instructor for either myself or my children. My husband is much esteemed among his religious acquaintance as a respectable Christian character, but his example at home is far from being delightful. Affable, condescending, and pleasing in the parlours of religious friends, but frequently either trifling and unsavoury, or imperious and unsocial in his own family. Preferring the opportunity of being entertained at a plentiful table, and of conversing with the wealthy, the polite, and the sprightly to the homely fare of his own family, and the company of his wife and children, he often spends his afternoons and evenings from home, until so late an hour that domestic worship is either omitted, or performed in a hasty and slovenly manner, with scarcely the appearance of devotion. Little caring for my soul, or for the management of our growing offspring, he seems concerned for hardly anything

15

more than keeping fair with his people; relative to which I have often calmly remonstrated and submissively entreated, but all in vain. Surrounded with little ones, and attended with straits, destitute of the sympathies, the instructions, the consolations which might have been expected from the affectionate heart of a pious husband, connected with the gifts of an evangelical minister, I pour out my soul to God, and mourn in secret."

Such, there is ground of apprehension, has been the sorrowful soliloquy of many a minister's pious, dutiful, and prudent wife. Take heed, then, to the best interests of your *Second-Self*.

To this end, except on extraordinary occasions, when impelled by duty, *spend your evenings at home*. Yes, and at an early hour in the evening, let your family and your study receive their demands on your presence in the lively performance of social and secret devotion. Thus, there will be reason to hope that domestic order and sociability, the improvement of your own understanding, and communion with God, will all be promoted.

Guard habitually against every appearance of imprudent intercourse and every indelicate familiarity with the most virtuous and pious of your female friends. Be particularly cautious of paying frequent visits to any single woman who lives alone; otherwise, your conduct may soon fall under the suspicion of your neighbours and also of your own wife, so as to become her daily tormentor, even while she believes you innocent of the great transgression. In cases of this kind, it is not sufficient that conscience bears witness to the purity of your conduct and the piety of your motives. For in matters of such a delicate nature, there should not be the least shadow of a ground either to support suspicion or to excite surmise. There is need for us, my brother, to watch and pray against the greatest sins—even against those to which, perhaps, we never perceived ourselves to be much inclined. For, alas, we have sometimes heard of apparently pious and evangelical ministers falling into such enormous crimes as not only disgrace religion, but degrade humanity.

Of late, I have been much affected with the following reflection:

> "Though, if not greatly deceived, I have had some degree of experimental acquaintance with Jesus Christ for almost forty years; though I have borne the ministerial character for upwards of twenty-five years; though I have been, perhaps, of some little use in the church of God; and though I have had a greater share of esteem among religious people than I had any reason to expect; yet, after all, it is possible for me, in one single hour of temptation, to blast my character—to ruin my public usefulness—and to render my warmest Christian friends ashamed of owning me. Hold thou me up, O Lord, and I shall be safe!"[5]

Ah, brother, there is little reason for any of us to be high-minded. And therefore, "happy is the man that feareth always" (Pro. 28:14).

---

[5] [The source of the quote is unknown.]

─────

7. Take heed to yourself with regard to the diligent improvement of your talents and opportunities in the whole course of your ministry. It behoves you, as a public teacher, to spend much of your time in reading and in study. Of this you are convinced and will act, I trust, agreeably to that conviction. For suitable means must be used, not only in your public ministry, in season and out of season, for the good of others, but with a view to the improvement of your own mind in an acquaintance with divine truth. Yes, my Christian friend, this is necessary, that your ability to feed the flock with knowledge and understanding may be increased, that your own heart may be more deeply tinctured with evangelical principles, that you may be the better prepared for every branch of pastoral duty and for every trying event that may occur.

For who can reasonably deny the necessity of diligence in the use of means adapted respectively to promote your own ministerial improvement and to obtain the great objects of your pastoral office, any more than to a rational prospect of success in the management of secular business? Be then as careful to improve opportunities of both obtaining and imparting spiritual benefits as the prudent and assiduous tradesman or mechanic is to promote the legitimate designs of his professional calling.

If a minister of the gospel behave with Christian decorum, possess tolerable abilities for his work, and, having his heart in it, be habitually industrious, there is reason to conclude that, in the common course of providence, he shall not labour in vain. As nobody, however, wonders that a merchant or a manufacturer who, having no pleasure in his employment, neglects his affairs and behaves as if he thought himself above his business, does not succeed but becomes bankrupt, so if a minister be seldom any further engaged, either in the study of truth or in the public exercises of religion than seems necessary to his continuance with decency in the pastoral station, there is no reason to wonder if his public devotion be without savour and his preaching without success. The church of which such a minister is the pastor seems completely warranted to cry in his ears, "Take heed to the ministry which thou hast received in the Lord, that thou fulfil it" (Col. 4:17; compare chapter 1:2).

———

8. Take heed to yourself respecting the motives by which you are influenced in all your endeavours to obtain useful knowledge. For if you read and study chiefly that you may cut a respectable figure in the pulpit, or to obtain and increase popular applause, the motive is carnal, base, and unworthy a man of God. Yet detestable in the sight of Him who searches the heart as that motive is, there will be the greatest necessity for you to guard against it as a besetting evil. It is perhaps as hard for a minister habitually to read and study with becoming diligence without being under this corrupt influence as it is for a tradesman prudently to manage a lucrative business without seeking the gratification of a covetous disposition. Yet both the minister and the tradesman must either guard against these pernicious evils or be in danger of sinking in final ruin.

Besides, whatever be the motives which principally operate in your private studies, it is highly probable those very motives will have their influence in the pulpit. If, when secretly studying the word of God, it was your chief concern to know the divine will that you might, with integrity and benevolence, lay it before your people for their benefit, it is likely the same holy motive will attend you in public service. But if a thirst of popularity or a lust of applause had the principal influence in the choice of your subject and in your meditations upon it, there will be no reason for surprise if you should be under the same detestable bias when performing your public labour.

Study your discourses, therefore, with a devotional disposition. To this you are bound by the very nature of the case as a Christian minister. For when the Bible is before you, it is the word of God on which you meditate and the work of God you are preparing to perform. It is reported of Dr. Cotton Mather,[6]

> "That in studying and preparing them, he would endeavour to make even that an exercise of devotion for his own soul. Accordingly his way was, at the end of every paragraph, to make a pause, and endeavour to make his own soul feel some holy impression of the truths contained in it. This he thought would be an excellent means of delivering his sermons with life and

---

[6] [Cotton Mather (1663-1728) was a prominent Puritan Congregationalist in colonial New England. The son of minister Increase Mather, he wrote and pastored at Old North Meeting House in Boston.]

spirit, and warming the hearts of his people by them: and so he found it. "[7]

It is, indeed, an easy thing for a preacher to make loud professions of regard to the glory of God and the good of immortal souls as the ruling motive in his ministerial conduct. But experience has taught me that it is extremely difficult for any minister to act suitably to such professions. For, as that pride which is natural to our species impels the generality of mankind to wish for eminence rather than usefulness in this or the other station, so it is with ministers of the Word. Forty years ago, I saw but little need of this caution compared with that conviction of its necessity which I now have. A preacher of the real gospel, I am fully persuaded, may appear exceedingly earnest and very faithful in his public labours as if his only design were to promote the cause of truth, the happiness of men, and the honour of God, while, nevertheless, he is more concerned to figure away at the head of a large body of people in the religious world than to advance the genuine interests of Jesus Christ and the felicity of his fellow mortals. What is it but this detestable pride that makes any of us ministers take more pleasure in perceiving our labours made useful to the rich, the learned, and the polite than to the poor, the illiterate, and the vulgar? It is, I presume, principally because it adds consequence to our own characters to have wealthy, well-educated, and polished persons in our churches. Jesus, however,

---

[7] Abridgement of Dr. C. Mather's Life, p. 38. [Samuel Mather, *An Abridgment of the Life of the Late Reverend and Learned Dr. Cotton Mather*, ed. David Jennings (London: Printed for J. Oswald, 1744), 38.]

in the time of his personal ministry, was far from being influenced by any such motive and equally far from showing the least predilection for persons of promising dispositions on any such grounds. Witness his behaviour to Nicodemus, to the young ruler, and to the nobleman at Capernaum (John 3:1–12; Mark 10:17–22; John 4:46–50).

I will add, what is it but the same depravity of heart which frequently renders us much more attentive to our wealthy friends than we are to our poor brethren in times of affliction, even though we be well assured that there is little danger of the rich being overlooked in their sorrows? Hoary as I now am in the ministry, and accustomed as I have been to hear conscience cry out against me for this, that, and the other omission of duty, I do not recollect that it ever charged me with neglecting any person in plentiful circumstances when deeply afflicted and requesting my visits. But, alas! I do recollect having frequently heard conscience, with a frowning aspect and an angry tone, either demanding, "Wouldst thou be thus backward to undergo some little inconvenience in visiting a wealthy patient?" or declaring, "That afflicted brother would not, through mere forgetfulness, have been recently disappointed of thy presence, conversation, and prayers, had he not been an obscure and a poor man. Had he been less deserving of thy compassionate regard, he would have been favoured with it." Alas, my brother, there is reason to fear that few ministers, on this ground, stand perfectly free from censure at the bar of a tender conscience!

As you should take heed to yourself respecting the principles on which you act and the ends at which you aim in your preparations for the pulpit, so it behoves you to be still more careful in these respects when you enter on public service. For then you professedly appear as a guilty creature to adore at the feet of Eternal Majesty, as a minister of the divine Jesus to perform his work, and as the servant of this church to promote the happiness of all its members. Endeavour, therefore, always to enter your pulpit under the force of this conviction: "I am an apostate creature and going to worship the omniscient God; a wretch who deserves to perish, yet looking to sovereign mercy; a sinner called by the gospel and trusting in the great atonement; confessedly insufficient for the work on which I am entering, but relying on the aids of grace." This will produce deep solemnity tempered with devout delight, which mixture of holy awe and sacred pleasure should accompany the Christian, and especially the Christian minister, whenever he approaches the Supreme.

Remarkable and important is that saying, "Let us have grace, whereby we may serve God acceptably with reverence and godly fear, for our God is a consuming fire" (Heb. 12:28–29). Very observable also is the language of David: "I will go to the altar of God, to God my exceeding joy" (Psa. 43:4). May the import of these passages, united, exert its force on your very soul whenever you take the lead in public worship! Then your graces as a Christian and your gifts as a minister will be exercised at the same time. Your graces being excited, you have communion with God; your gifts being exerted, the people are edified. Whereas, were you to enter the pulpit merely to exercise your ministerial talents, though others might be fed by the truths delivered, your own soul would starve. This, I fear, is the case of many who preach the gospel.

But what a figure, in the eye of Omniscience, must that preacher make who is not habitually desirous of exercising devout affections in the performance of his public work! Like an index on the high road, he directs others in the way to heaven, but he walks not in it himself. He may prophesy with Balaam or preach with Judas; his learning and knowledge, his natural parts and spiritual gifts may excite admiration and be useful to others, but, being destitute of internal devotion, his heart is not right with God, and he is a wretched creature. "Sounding brass or a tinkling cymbal" (1 Cor. 13:1) is the character by which he is known in sacred Scripture.

When, however, commencing public service, it is needful to remember that you appear not only as a worshipper of God, but as a minister of Christ. Being such, it is your indispensable duty to preach Christ, and not yourself; that is, with sincerity and ardour, to aim at displaying the glories of his person and the riches of his grace, the spirituality of his kingdom and the excellence of his government—not your own ingenuity or eloquence, your parts or learning. Guard, then, my brother, as against the most pernicious evil; guard, as for your very life, against converting the gospel ministry into a vehicle to exhibit your own excellence, or prostituting the doctrine of Christ crucified to the gratification of your pride, or that it may be a pander to your praise. For who can estimate the magnitude of that guilt which is included in such conduct? Yet, with this enormous and horrible evil, I cannot forbear suspecting many ministers are more or less chargeable. Nay, to the commission of this outrage on the honour of Christ and of grace, every minister should consider himself as liable. For so polluted are our hands that, without grace preventing, we defile everything we touch. So depraved are our hearts that we are in danger of committing a robbery on the glory of our divine Lord, even when it is our professed business to exalt it.

As, when entering on public devotion, you should endeavour to act becoming your character under the notion of a guilty creature in audience with the King Eternal, and as a minister of Christ, whose business it is to display his glory, so you are further to consider yourself as the servant of this church. When standing up to address your people, it should ever be with an earnest desire of promoting their happiness. They, having chosen you to the pastoral office, you having accepted their invitation, and being now solemnly ordained to the important service, that mutual agreement and the interesting transactions of this day should operate as a threefold motive to the faithful performance of your public work. Yes, you are bound affectionately to aim at doing them good by laying divine truth before them in such a manner as is adapted to enlighten their minds, to affect their hearts, and to promote their edification.

Though the occasional exercise of your ministerial talents in other places may be both lawful and commendable, yet, as it is here only that you stand in the pastoral relation, you ought, except in extraordinary cases, to fill this pulpit yourself and not leave the deacons to procure supplies in a precarious manner while you are serving some other community. It is here, as a public teacher, that your proper business lies, and here, at the usual times of assembling, your voice must be heard. When the pastor of a church discovers an inclination to avail himself of almost any pretext for being absent from his people in order to serve others, he gives reason of suspicion, whatever his pretences may be, that either filthy lucre or a lust of popularity has too much place in his heart, and that he accepted the pastoral office rather as an article of convenience than as matter of duty. It is, indeed, much to be lamented that, though Dissenting Ministers in general justly exclaim against the non-residence and the holding of pluralities which are so common among the clergy, yet the conduct of some pastors among the Nonconformists makes near approaches to that of pluralities in our National Establishment and is a violation of pastoral duty.

You should seek, with peculiar care, to obtain the approbation of conscience in each of your hearers, as appears by the following words, "By manifestation of the truth, commending ourselves to every man's conscience in the sight of God" (2 Cor. 4:2). This illustrious passage presents us with a view of Paul in the pulpit, and a very solemn appearance he makes.

He has just been adoring in secret at the feet of the Most High, and, recent from converging with the Most Holy, he is now going to address his fellow sinners. Penetrated with the importance of his office and the solemnity of his present situation, he manifestly feels—he seems to tremble. Nor need we wonder, for the subject on which he is to speak, the object he has in view, and the witness of his conduct, are all interesting and solemn to the last degree. Truth, conscience, and God—the most important and impressive thoughts that can enter the human mind—pervade his very soul. Evangelical truth is the subject of his discussion, the approbation of conscience is the object of his desire, and the omniscient Holy One is the witness of his conduct. An example, this, which you, and I, and every minister of the word are bound to imitate. Make it your diligent endeavour, then, to obtain the approbation of conscience from all that hear you, for without deserving that, none of your public labours can be to your honour or turn to your own account in the great day of the Lord.

A minister may say things that are profoundly learned and very ingenious, that are uncommonly pretty and extremely pleasing to the generality of his hearers, without aiming to reach their consciences and to impress their hearts, either by asserting divine authority or by displaying divine grace. When this is the case, he obtains, it may be, from superficial hearers the reward which he sought, for he is greatly admired and applauded. But, alas! the unawakened sinner is not alarmed, the hungry soul is not fed, and the Father of mercies is defrauded

27

of that reverence and confidence, of that love and obedience, which a faithful declaration of the gracious and sanctifying truth might have produced. Yes, my brother, it is much to be suspected that many ministers have recommended themselves to the fancies, the tastes, the affections of their hearers, who never deserved and who never had, in a serious hour, the approbation of their consciences.

Be ambitious, therefore, of obtaining and preserving the suffrage of conscience in your favour, whether admired and honoured with verbal applause or not. For it is evident from observation that a preacher who is endued with a competent share of learning and fine parts, a retentive memory and good elocution, may recommend himself to the admiration of great numbers, while their consciences, in the hour of solemn reflection, bear testimony against him. Because, as a minister may have all those engaging qualifications, while habitually proud and covetous, deceitful and vain, so the conscience never feels itself interested in the fine imagination, the genius, or the learning which a minister discovers in his public services. It is worthy of remark, my brother, that though none of us can command success to our labours, were we ever so pious, diligent, and faithful, and though it may not be in our power to obtain the applause of literature, of genius, or of address, yet, in the common course of things, if we be assiduous, benevolent, and upright in our labours, we may secure the approbation of conscience in the generality of our stated hearers, which is an article of great importance to the tranquillity of a minister's own breast.

Now, my young friend, if you keep conscience in view, if you remember that God himself is a witness of your latent motives and of your public labours, you will not choose an obscure text principally that you may have the honour of explaining it, nor will you select one which has no relation to the subject you mean to discuss in order that your acumen may shine by making it speak what it never thought. The more you keep the approbation of conscience and the presence of God in your eye, the more dependent will you be on divine assistance in all your ministerial addresses. Yes, bearing in mind, on every occasion of this kind, that your business here is to plead for the interests of evangelical truth under the immediate inspection of him who is *the truth*. You cannot but feel your incapacity and look for assistance to God, whose cause you mean to promote. The more you keep the consciences of men and the presence of God in your view, the more will you be impressed with the importance of your subject, and the more earnest will you be in addressing your hearers, for that minister must have a strange set of passions who does not feel himself roused by such considerations. The more you keep the approbation of conscience and the inspection of God in remembrance, the less will you be disposed to indulge a light and trifling spirit, and the more devotional will you be in the course of your administrations, for the ordinances of God are too sacred to become the vehicles of entertainment, and His presence is too solemn to permit the smile of levity.

Keeping the consciences of men and the Searcher of hearts in view, it will afford you much more pleasure to find that persons who have been hearing you left the place bemoaning their apostate state and very deeply abased before the Most Holy, than to be informed that they greatly admired you as a preacher and loudly applauded your ministerial talents. Because, for a person to depart from public worship in raptures with the minister's abilities is no proof that he has received any spiritual benefit. But if, smitten with a sense of guilt, he cry out, "How shall I escape the wrath to come? God be merciful to me a sinner!" (Luke 18:13). Or if he exclaim, "Who is a god like unto our God? How great is his goodness, and how great is his beauty! What shall I render to the Lord for all his benefits?" (Mic. 7:18; Psa. 116:12), then it looks as if the preacher had commended himself to his conscience and as if the truth had reached his heart. For language of this kind from a reflecting hearer has a devotional aspect and gives glory to God. It indicates a soul either as being apprehensive of deserved ruin, or as rejoicing in revealed mercy; as having a good hope through grace, or as revering divine authority. Whereas barely to admire and praise the preacher is quite consistent with reigning depravity and with rooted enmity to God. As it is written, "They sit before thee as my people, and they hear thy words— With their mouth they show much love, but their heart goeth after their covetousness. And lo, thou art unto them as a very lovely song of one that hath a pleasant voice, and can play well on an instrument; for they hear thy words, but they do them not" (Eze. 33:31–32).

Once more, in proportion as the approbation of conscience and the inspection of God are properly kept in view, the pleasure you have arising from verbal commendations of professed friends, and the pain of strong opposition from the avowed enemies of evangelical truth, will be diminished. For conscience does not often express itself in the language of noisy applause, which, when free from hypocrisy, is commonly the fruit of a weak understanding under the influence of strong passions. Hence, it is not unfrequent for those who have been the most liberal in praising a minister to be found among the first who entirely desert his ministry. As to unfounded censures and violent opposition, the testimony of a good conscience and the countenance of Scripture are adapted to afford the needful support.

---

9. Take heed to yourself with regard to that success and those discouragements which may attend your ministry. Should a large degree of apparent success, through the favour of heaven, accompany your labours, there will be the highest necessity to guard against pride and self-esteem. A young man of good ministerial abilities and honoured with great usefulness is in a delicate situation respecting the prosperity of his own soul. For, through the want of experience and observation, such concurrence of pleasing particulars has proved to some very promising characters the innocent occasion of disgrace and ruin. Shining abilities and a blessing upon their labours have rendered them popular. Popularity has intoxicated them with pride. Pride has exposed them to various temptations. Temptations have prevailed and either precipitated them into some enormous offence, or laid the foundation of a gradual departure from the truth and from the practice of real piety. If the former, their character has been killed as by the stroke of an apoplexy. If the latter, their comfort and usefulness have been destroyed as by a consuming hectic.[8] Agreeable to that saying, "Pride goeth before destruction, and a haughty spirit before a fall" (Pro. 16:18).

Remember, therefore, my brother, that though it is your indispensable duty to labour and pray for prosperity in your work, yet a season of remarkable success will generally prove an hour of peculiar temptation to your own soul. Take heed to yourself at such a time and watch the secret motions of your own heart. The number of your hearers may increase, and your church may flourish, while in your own breast devotional affections and virtuous dispositions are greatly on the decline. Nor need I inform you that every degree of such declension has a tendency to final ruin.

Besides, if there should be an appearance of extensive utility attending your labours, for which I sincerely pray, you may do well to remember the old proverb, "All is not gold that glitters." Numbers there are that seem to receive the word with

---

[8] *Si minister verbi laudatur, versatur in periculo,* says the famous Augustine. [English: If the minister of the word is praised, he is in danger.]

joy, who in time of temptation fall away (Luke 8:13). Many evangelical and popular preachers, I am very suspicious, have greatly over-rated the usefulness of their own labours. For the longer I live, the more apprehensive I am that the number of real converts among those who profess the genuine gospel is comparatively very small, according to the import of that alarming declaration, "Many are called, but few are chosen" (Matt. 22:14).

On the other hand, should you meet with many and great discouragements, take heed that you do not indulge a desponding temper as if you had been of no use in the ministerial work. With discouragements you certainly will meet unless Providence were to make your case an exception to the general course of things, which you have no ground to expect. Very painful discouragements, for instance, may sometimes arise from the want of liberty and savour in your own mind when performing public service. This, there is reason to suppose, is not uncommon. I, at least, have had frequent experience of it; and once, to such a degree, that I began to think very seriously of giving up the ministry, supposing that the Great Shepherd had nothing further for me to do, either in the pastoral office or in preaching the word at large. This exercise of mind, though exceedingly painful for some weeks, was both instructive and useful. Before that well-recollected season, I had frequently talked about the necessity of divine influence to render a minister savoury in his own mind, as well as profitable to others, but then I *felt* it.

Be not discouraged, then, as though some strange thing happened unto you that never befel a real minister of Christ, if a similar trial should occur in the course of your ministry. For it may be to you, as I trust it was to me, of no inconsiderable benefit, because I reckon that whatever curbs our pride makes us feel our insufficiency and sends us to the throne of grace. Seldom, alas! have I found any remarkable degree of savour and of enlargement in public service without experiencing, more or less, self-elatement and self-gratulation on that account. Instead of complaining, therefore, that I have not more liberty in my work or more success attending the performance of it, I have reason to wonder at the condescending kindness of God in that he gives to my extremely imperfect labours the least saving effect, and that he does not frequently leave me to be confounded before all my hearers. Such, brother, have been the feelings and reasonings of my own mind, and such my confessions before God many a time.

It is not unlikely that in a course of years some of your people who had expressed a warm regard to your ministry, and perhaps considered you as their spiritual father, may become, without any just reason, your violent opposers, asperse your ministerial character, and wish to be rid of you. This, though very trying, is far from an unexampled case—no, not with regard to much greater men and far better ministers than either of us. Witness the language of Paul in various parts of his two epistles to the Church at Corinth and in his letter to the Galatian churches. Witness also the life of that excellent man,

Mr. President Edwards of New England.[9]

Among the dissatisfied it is probable some will complain of your ministry being dry, legal, and of an Arminian cast, while others, it may be, will quarrel with it under a supposition that you dwell too much on the doctrines of divine grace and verge toward Antinomianism. My own ministry, however, has been the subject of loud complaint in these opposite ways, and that at the very same time. Nor have we much reason to wonder at it. For if a minister, to the best of his ability, display the glory of sovereign grace in the election, redemption, and justification of sinners, he will be sure to offend the pride of multitudes who are seeking acceptance with God by their own obedience. Persons of this character will probably draw the same inferences from his doctrine and form the same objections against it as those by which the ministry of Paul was opposed. If it be so, they will cry, "Why does God yet find fault? for who hath resisted his will? Let us do evil that good may come, and continue in sin, that grace may abound. The law is made void, and personal holiness is quite superfluous" (Rom. 3:8; 6:1; 9:19).

Does the same preacher insist upon the necessity of that holiness, without which no one shall see the Lord (Heb. 12:14)—upon that conformity to the example of Christ, and that spiritual-mindedness, without which all pretensions to faith in the Son of God are vain? The covetousness and

[9] [Jonathan Edwards (1703–1758) was one of the great theologians of the First Great Awakening in America. His voluminous writings and preaching sparked revivals in Northampton, MA and beyond. In 1750 he was dismissed from his church after experiencing great ministry there. You can read more about it in George M. Marsden, *Jonathan Edwards: A Life* (New Haven: Yale University Press, 2004).]

carnality of others will be disgusted. They will pronounce him legal and consider his doctrine as inimical to the prerogatives of sovereign grace; and this because he maintains that evangelical truths have a holy influence on all who believe them, or, in the language of James, that faith without works is dead (Jas. 2:17).

Again, you may, it is highly probable, have painful opportunities of observing that while some of your people embrace pernicious doctrines, verge to wide extremes, and are exceedingly desirous of making proselytes to their novel peculiarities, others of them are giddy and flighty, rambling about from one place of worship to another, admiring almost every fresh preacher they hear, but quite dissatisfied with your ministry, though they hardly know for what. Nor is there any reason to doubt that others among the objects of your pastoral care will administer occasions of grief by formality and lukewarmness in their profession, by their pride, extravagance, or sensuality, by their envy, avarice, or injustice, or finally by malevolent attacks, in unfounded charges upon your own character, as in the case of Paul among the Corinthians. You must guard, however, against desponding discouragement when any of these painful particulars occur to your notice. Nay, should a variety of them appear at the same time, you must not conclude that God has deserted your ministry and entirely forsaken your church. But, while firmly determined to promote the exercise of strict and impartial discipline and while careful, except the case be quite peculiar, never to bring the bad conduct of any individual into your public discourses, examine your own ways—humble yourself before God (2 Cor. 12:20–21), increase your pastoral exertions, cry mightily to the Father of mercies for assistance, endeavour, as it were, to *levy a tax* upon these trials that they may, at least, afford private advantage to your own soul (Rom. 8:28), and then, leaving your cause with God, *be of good courage*.

I said, *endeavour to levy a tax upon your trials.* For even malevolent attacks and unfounded charges upon a Christian's character, if his own temper be under proper government, may prove an occasion of promoting his best interests. In such cases and for this end, it behoves him to examine his heart and ways to see whether he have not contracted the guilt of some greater evil than that which is falsely laid to his charge. If on impartial inquiry his conscience attest the affirmative, it will soon appear that he has much less reason to redden with indignation at his accuser's unfounded charge than he has to admire the goodness of God in permitting an arrow to be aimed at his character which he can easily repel by the impenetrable shield of a good conscience, while greater evils of his heart or conduct, for which he cannot but severely condemn himself, are entirely hidden from his accuser. Besides, the Christian, in such a predicament, may justly say, "Though free from the charge alleged, it is not owing to the superior holiness of my heart, but must be ascribed to divine preserving care."

A Christian, therefore, who in such a conjuncture of circumstances is wisely seeking his own emolument, will be disposed to consider the unrighteous allegation as a gracious providential warning, lest at any time he be really overtaken of that very evil with which, at present, he is falsely accused. Little do we know of the spiritual danger to which we are continually exposed, the temptations by which we may be unawares powerfully assaulted, or how near we may be to the perpetration of some awful evil from which we have commonly imagined ourselves to be most remote. Neither, on the other hand, is it possible for us thoroughly to understand all the ways and means by which our heavenly Father communicates those hidden provisions of preventing grace which are continually administered for our preservation.[10] But, alas! how seldom it is that any of us have humility and wisdom sufficient thus to improve such an event!

―――――

Once more, *10. Take heed that you pay an habitual regard to divine influence, as that without which you cannot either enjoy a holy liberty in your work or have any reason to expect success.* We have heard with pleasure that the necessity of such an influence to enlighten, to comfort, and to sanctify the human mind makes one article in your theological creed—an article, doubtless, of great importance. For as well might the material system have sprung out of nonentity without the almighty fiat as an assemblage of holy qualities arise in a depraved heart without supernatural agency. As well might

---

[10] Dr. Owen's Sermons and Tracts, p. 49.

the order, harmony, and beauty of the visible world be continued without the perpetual exertion of that wisdom, power, and goodness which gave them birth as the holy qualities of a regenerate soul be maintained and flourish independent of the Divine Spirit.

Now, my brother, as the knowledge of any truth is no further useful to us than we are influenced by it and act upon it—as doctrinal sentiments are not beneficial except in proportion as they become practical principles or produce correspondent feelings and affections in our own hearts—so you should endeavour to live continually under the operation of that sacred maxim, "Without *me* ye can do nothing" (John 15:5). With humility, with prayer, and with expectation, the assistance of the Holy Spirit should be daily regarded. In all your private studies and in all your public administrations, the aids of that Sacred Agent should be sought. Consistency of conduct, peace in your own breast, and success in your own labours all require it, for surely you do not mean merely to compliment the Holy Spirit by giving his work a conspicuous place in your creed. Were you habitually to study and preach your discourses without secret previous prayer for divine assistance, the criminality of your neglect would equal the inconsistency of your character. If Christianity be the religion of sinners and adapted to their apostate state, it must provide as well for our depravity by enlightening and sanctifying influence as for our guilt by atoning blood.

Our Lord, when addressing his disciples relative to the

gracious work of the Holy Spirit, says, "He shall glorify me, for he shall receive of mine and shall show it unto you" (John 16:14). By which, we are led to infer that when a minister sincerely seeks and mercifully obtains divine assistance in preaching the Word, his discourses will have a sweet savour of Christ and his offices will display his mediatorial glories, will exhibit his excellent characters and condescending relations that are suited to the necessities of miserable sinners. Thus, he will feast the mental eye and excite admiration of the Saviour's person and undertaking in the believing heart, even though the elocution and manner of the preacher be of an inferior kind. Hence you may learn, my brother, how to appreciate those discourses which, whether heard from the pulpit or perused from the press, frequently excite admiration of the minister's talents but are far from raising the same passion to an equal degree by exhibiting the personal and official excellencies of the adorable Jesus.

Nor can you pray over your Bible in a proper manner when meditating on the sacred text without feeling a solemnity in your ministerial employment. That solemnity should always attend you in the pulpit, for a preacher who trifles there not only affronts the understanding of every sensible and serious hearer but insults the majesty of that Divine Presence in which he stands. Guard, therefore, against every appearance of levity in your public work. In all your studies and in all your labours watch against a spirit of self-sufficiency from which that profane levity often proceeds. Remember that your ability for

40

every spiritual duty and all your success must be from God. To him your eye must be directed and on his promised aid your expectations of usefulness must be formed. In thus acting the part of a Christian, while you perform the work of a minister for the benefit of others your own soul will feel itself interested in the doctrines you preach and in the duties you inculcate, in the promises you exhibit and in the reproofs you administer.

I will now, my brother, for a few minutes, direct your attention to another divine precept, and then conclude. Paul, when addressing Titus in the language of apostolic authority, says, "Let no one despise thee" (Tit. 2:15). A singular and remarkable saying! No one, whether a professed Christian, an unbelieving Jew, or an idolatrous Gentile. Observe, however, it is not said, "Let no one envy, or hate, or persecute thee," but let no one *despise* thee. How then was Titus to preserve his character from contempt? By the penal exercise of miraculous powers on those who dared to treat him with indignity? No such expedient is here intimated. By assuming lordly titles, appearing in splendid robes, taking to himself state, and causing the vulgar to keep their distance? Nothing less. For that would have been directly contrary to an established law of Christ and inconsistent with the nature of his kingdom. But it was, as the apostle in another place plainly intimates, by becoming a bright example of the believers—in word, in conversation, in charity or love, in spirit, in faith or fidelity, in purity (1 Tim. 4:12), or by being pre-eminent among those who adorned the doctrine of God our Saviour (Tit. 2:10).

Yes, a minister of the gospel who takes heed to himself—to his Christian character, to his official duties, and to his various relations in life, whether domestic, religious, or civil—is not very likely to be sincerely despised by those that know him. His supposed religious oddities may be treated with contempt, and he may be hated for his conscientious regard to evangelical truth and to the legislative authority of Jesus Christ, but the manifest respectability of his moral character will find an advocate in the breast of each that knows him, and especially in the hour of serious reflection. For, a series of conduct bearing testimony to the reality of religious principle, to the fear of God, and to the social virtues reigning in his heart, will generally secure him from deliberate contempt. Hence, it has been observed by an author of eminence[11] in his literary station: "It was a pertinent advice that Paul gave to [Titus], however oddly it may appear at first: Let no one despise thee. For we may justly say, that in ninety-nine cases out of a hundred, if a pastor is despised, he has himself to blame."[12]

Yes, and how respectable soever for literature and science, if he entered upon his office chiefly under the influence of secular motives, or if he be habitually trifling and vain, proud or covetous, if in his general conduct there be more of the modern fine gentleman than of the primitive pastor, and much more of the man of this world than of the man of God, he

---

[11] [Dr. George Campbell (1719–1796) was a Scottish minister and professor of divinity at Marischal College, Aberdeen. He was a prolific writer and founding member of the Royal Society of Edinburgh.]

[12] Dr. G. Campbell's Lectures on Ecclesiastical History, vol. 1, p. 174. [George Campbell, D.D., *Lectures on Ecclesiastical History*, vol. 1 (London: Printed for J. Johnson, 1800), 174.]

deserves, under the pastoral character, to be despised. For the feelings and sympathies and turn of his heart are neither congenial to those of the Great Shepherd, under whom he should serve, and with whom, in order to feed the flock, he must have frequent spiritual intercourse, nor adapted to meet the necessities of any people that know the Chief Pastor's voice (John 10:4). He is a man of the world, and, as such, a Cure in the National Establishment seems more congenial to him than a pastoral charge among the Dissenters. For a Protestant Dissenting Minister who is not above the world is very likely to be despised by the world.

Take heed, then, my brother, that no one may have any reason to despise you, and that this church may never, like the church at Colosse, come under the obligation of that precept, "Say to Archippus, take heed to the ministry which thou hast received in the lord that thou fulfil it" (Col. 4:17). An apostolic injunction this, which it is to be feared, attaches to many churches respecting their lukewarm and negligent pastors. Nay, who that is daily lamenting over the plague of his own heart, that reflects on the state of religion in what is called the Christian world, that considers the ministerial work and the pastoral office as being both sacred and important, and finally that demand of the Supreme Judge, give an account of thy stewardship, can forbear to acknowledge the propriety of Dr. Owen's pathetic language when he says, "The Lord help men, and open their eyes before it be too late! For, either the Gospel is not true, or there are few who, in a due manner, discharge that ministry which they take upon them."[13]

———

11. Take heed, I once more charge you: take heed to yourself. This duty performed, you can scarcely forbear taking heed either to the doctrine you preach or to the flock over which the Holy Ghost hath made you an overseer to feed the church of God, which He hath purchased with His own blood. AMEN.

---

[13] On Epist. to the Hebrews, chap. 6:11, vol. 3, p. 118. Folio. [John Owen, *An Exposition of the Epistle to the Hebrews*, vol. 3, 2nd ed. (London: Printed for James Black, 1815), 182.]

www.ingramcontent.com/pod-product-compliance
Lightning Source LLC
LaVergne TN
LVHW041237080426
835508LV00011B/1250